LET'S TALK ABOUT IT!

THE BOOK FOR CHILDREN ABOUT CHILD ABUSE

by

Dr. Michael L. Pall
and
Lois Blackburn Streit

Published by
R & E Publishers
P. O. Box 2008
Saratoga, California 95070

Library of Congress Card Catalog Number
82-60527

I.S.B.N.
0-88247-682-3

DEDICATION

"To our parents who have shown us the way.
To our children who will carry it on."

ACKNOWLEDGEMENTS

We wish to thank Charlotte Pall who assisted greatly in the preparation of this book for publication, and the following non-abused children for their assistance in reviewing the materials for this book: Ashli Brown, Mark Facklam, Matthew Jones; and Robin, Sara, Elizabeth and Rachel Streit.

We would also like to thank our colleagues at the clinic and in the community for their interest and support.

CONTENTS

INTRODUCTION

Child Abuse and Neglect is a very serious problem which touches us all. Obviously, it is a problem for the children who are abused and neglected. Perhaps less obviously it is a problem for the abusing parents, who themselves are most often grown-up, abused children, and for their families. Since the family unit is the basic building block of the community, it is also a community problem.

We wrote this book for children, and also for parents. We hope that after reading it, abused children and abusing parents will have a better understanding of why they feel the way they do, do some of the things they do, and consider what they can do to stop the hurting. After reading this book, we hope that children who are not abused, and parents who are not abusing, have a greater understanding of feelings and behaviors in general; of the problem of child abuse and neglect, and of how they can help to solve the problem.

In addition to children and their parents, we hope that

other members of the community will find this book helpful. Teachers and other school personnel can use this book in classroom discussions of family life, parenting skills and in units on social problems.

Child Protective Workers might use this book for training and staff development, in explaining their roles to the general public, and of course, in working directly with abusing families.

As therapists, in addition to talking, we recognize the value of using written materials in the course of therapy with children and their families. We have, therefore, often felt the need for a resource such as this book. So, we wrote it.

CHAPTER I

WHAT IS CHILD ABUSE

I. Definitions:

Child Abuse — All parents sometimes do things which hurt their children's bodies or feelings. When a parent does something painful to a child it may be on purpose or by accident. The parent may want to cause the child pain (such as when parents spank children), or the pain may have to happen when parents do something for their children which needs to be done (such as cleaning out a scrape or a cut).

What then is child abuse? It is when parents or guardians (an adult acting as a parent) hurt their children's bodies or feelings over and over again — on purpose; and the only way such parents give attention is by yelling, hitting, or being angry. Again, it is important for

1

you to know that all parents hurt their children's bodies and feelings from time to time, either accidentally, or on purpose.

We know how parents may cause us pain on purpose, such as by yelling at us (which makes us feel scared and sad and angry), or by spanking. But how can they hurt us by accident, or when they don't want to? Have you ever wrestled with Dad or Mom for fun? Did you ever get hurt by accident while doing this? Or did they? Sometimes when we play we get hurt.

Other times Mom and Dad may hurt you in order to help you, as when they take care of that cut or scrape we spoke of, or when they give you the medicine the doctor ordered to make you feel better when you are sick. When the Doctor or Nurse gives you a "shot," it's because you need one to be well. It's not a punishment but it still hurts.

A parent may hurt your feelings by accident by teasing you, or calling you names, laughing at something you do or say, or by not seeing how important something is to you (like the new toy you wanted so much to have). But, if a parent hurts his children's feelings over and over again, and the only kind of attention parents give their children is the kind that makes them feel hurt, that is Child Abuse.

It is also child abuse if a parent or guardian uses children's bodies in a sexual way, or if a parent does not protect a child from being used in that way. Sexual abuse usually happens with a grown-up man and a girl child, or sometimes with a grown-up man or woman with

2

a boy child. If a grownup wants to see you undressed not just to give a bath, or for a checkup with the nurse or doctor), or wants to touch and feel you in "private" spots, or if a grownup wants to undress in front of you or have you touch him, this can be sexual abuse.

Child Neglect — This is when things DON'T happen to you, that most people agree should happen to ALL children. Such as:

1. *Lack of Supervision*: Parents can't spend all their time with you. They must sometimes be away from you, when they are at work, or when you are at school. It is important for them, also, to have time to be alone with grown-up friends, just as sometimes you may like to play alone with your friends. However, it is important for your parents to know where you are and that you are safe. So, if your parents cannot supervise you themselves, they ask another grownup, or older person, to supervise you for them (such as an aunt, grandmother, or a "sitter"). Supervision means that a grownup is close enough to you to help you if you need help of any kind, and that he knows where you are and that you are safe and when to expect you home when you've gone out.

Some parents, however, do not know where their children are, what they are doing, and if they are playing in a safe place in a safe way. Others may allow their children to return home very late at night. Or, they may go out and not let their children know where they are, when they will be back, or what the child can do if he

3

needs help of any kind. Again, while these things may happen from time to time in any family, when they happen over and over again it is called "lack of supervision," and it is a kind of Child Neglect.

2. *Lack of Protection:* As we talked about before, parents can't always protect (keep) you from getting hurt by accident. Almost all children and grownups have been, or will be, hurt by accident at some time in their lives. Some accidents can be prevented (kept from happening) when people correct (fix) situations in which accidents are likely to happen.

For example, if my car's windshield is so dirty that I can't see through it, will I be more or less likely to have an accident, or run into the car in front of me? If you said, "more likely," you are right! How could I lower the chances of this accident happening to me? If you said by "cleaning the windshield," you are right again!

Children who have accidents, which could have been made not to happen, and who have them over and over again, may have parents who are not protecting them enough. This is another kind of Child Neglect.

3. *Lack of Necessities for Life and Growth:* Necessities are things that all persons, children and grownups, need to live. Food, shelter (a safe place to live), and clothing are some necessities. So are education (school), and medical and dental care. Unfortunately, not everyone in this country gets the same amount of

necessities. How much food we get to eat, or how good it is; how many different types of clothing we have, or how big and nice our house is, depends on how much money the family has.

However, everyone can get enough food to live on, enough clothing to wear, and a place to live in; and it is expected that all children will be provided with these. This is so because, when parents cannot earn enough money to give their children these necessities, the government will give them through a system called "Public Assistance" or "Welfare." Parents must ASK the government for help, if it is needed, in order to get it. We'll talk about it a little more, later on in the book.

Sometimes, parents do not give their children enough food, or proper clothing, or a safe place in which to live. They never take them to a clinic or a hospital or a doctor when they are sick. They allow their children to "skip" school many times during a school year. By LAW you *must* go to school, even if you sometimes do not like it and your parents do not care if you miss school. They don't dress their children warmly enough in the winter and the children are often sick with colds. They don't see to it that their children wash and bathe. Again, it is when these things are happening over and over again that it is a kind of Child Neglect.

II.   Feelings and Behaviors:
       As humans we all have FEELINGS such as glad,

sad, mad and scared. Sometimes we show these feeling through BEHAVIORS such as crying (sad feeling), hitting (mad feeling), laughing (glad feeling), and others. Feelings are *inside* of us, and other people may not know what we are feeling unless we tell them. Or, they may guess these feelings we're having by watching the behaviors — how we act shows others how we feel. Sometimes, they may guess wrong. (Have you ever seen people cry when they say they are very happy? Did you think they were sad?)

Behaviors can be seen, described (talked about), and even counted by others. These are easier for others to describe because many times there is agreement among others as to what a behavior is. For example, we can all agree as to what a "home run" is in baseball. Therefore, we can also agree on which baseball player hit the most number of home runs, since records are kept of baseball playing behaviors (home runs, errors, walks, strikes, etc.) Do you know who hit the most number of home runs ever?

Sometimes, our parents use words to describe (tell about) behaviors which confuse us or mix us up. Words like "back-talk," "sassing," or "not minding," are often used to tell about children's behaviors which parents find annoying (they don't like them). However, these words are not the best way of describing behaviors since they may mean different things to different people. If you ask three children what "sassing" means, you may get three different definitions (meanings) or examples; but, if you ask them what a home run means, you will probably get only one definition. We will be talking about behaviors in a way that, we hope, most people will understand.

All the behaviors we talk about are shown by all people from time to time. However, as we said before, abused children and abusing parents show these behaviors much more of the time than children who have not been abused, and parents who are not abusers.

If you are, or have been abused by your parents, you may behave and feel much of the time in the following ways:

You may be VERY careful about the way you act with others, acting very cooperative and not asking for anything from others in return. You may have learned to "keep a low profile." That is, to avoid being punished by your parents you may have learned to have as little contact with them as possible, in order to stay safe. Since you are scared of your parents hurting you, you are also scared that others outside of your family will hurt you, too. You may feel that no one can be trusted; that others will hurt you if they can. So, to keep from being hurt, you must either stay away from everyone or just go along with everything they say or do.

You may, on the other hand, do a lot of fighting and NOT go along with anything others say or do. This may be because you are feeling so angry and mixed up at the way you have been treated by your parents. Sometimes your parents are loving and treat you in such a way that you feel good, like when they pay attention to you. Other times they may hurt you.

What may be mixing you up is that it doesn't seem to matter whether your BEHAVIOR is "good" or "bad."

7

Your parents may hurt you one time and make you feel good another time. When you feel angry and mixed-up about this, you may show these feelings by fighting, having "temper-tantrums," or by not being able to sit still.

Sometimes you may behave as if you were the parent and try to take care of your parents as if your parents were the children, since it seems that your parents want you to do this. Or, you may act much younger than you really are, since this seems to please your parents or make them feel good.

You may feel it is not okay to cry, to talk about your feelings, or even to be curious — to want to find out about things or explore.

If you have been hit a lot you may dislike it when people touch you. Even when they try to pat you on the head or give you a hug to show that they like you, again you may fear that other people outside of your family will hurt you the way your parents may have hurt you. On the other hand, you may try to act very, very friendly to strangers, feeling that they will give you the love your parents haven't.

You may feel that you must not allow yourself to play or have fun, because you feel that you are bad and do not deserve to feel good; or that grownups don't like it when you feel good.

We should talk here about the difference between FEELING that you are a bad person and behaving badly (that is, doing things which are bad). All of us do things which are bad, but most people are good people! Doing bad things sometimes doesn't mean a person is bad. Sometimes, very good people do some bad things.

For example, once, when I was stopped for a red light, I noticed a car go through the interesection against the red light. It should have stopped, but it didn't, and it just missed hitting another car! It did stop on the other side of the intersection and four nuns got out of the car. They told the driver of the car they had almost hit how sorry they were that they had gone through the red light and that they had scared him.

They explained that they had been talking and that they didn't notice that the light had turned red. Luckily, no one had been hurt, but they had broken the law and had done something wrong, or "bad." Their behavior might have caused them to be punished by being ticketed (having to pay a money fine), or not being allowed to drive a car for a time.

Now, most people would agree that nuns are good people, but they had done a bad thing. The point is, no matter how many bad behaviors you have done, you are not a bad person. You are a good person who has done some bad things.

Your parents, too, are probably good people, but they may have done many bad things (to you). Later on, we will talk about how your parents can change their behaviors, and how you can change yours.

It is important for you to know that the scared and angry feelings you may have, and the behaviors that we've talked about that you may use to express these feelings, can change at any time you want them to.

Your parents may also have very scared and angry feelings and they sometimes show these feelings by behaving in a way that hurts you. They may also feel that they are not good parents or even good people. They may show these feelings by not trusting others, not having many friends, and by saying that "most people are just no good." They may see you as different or "bad" because they see themselves that way and you are their children. Later, we will see how your parents got these feelings and how they can change their feelings and their behaviors towards you.

Again, it is most important for you to know that the scared and angry feelings your parents have, and the behaviors they show which hurt you, can change at any time if they want them to.

BOTH PARENTS ARE HURTING THEIR KIDS.
WHICH ONE IS DOING IT ON PURPOSE?
WHICH PARENT IS A CHILD ABUSER?

CHAPTER II

WHY IS IT HAPPENING?

Earlier we talked about the scared and angry feelings your parents may have and the way in which they may see themselves and you as "bad" people. We talked about how your parents may not trust other people, and feel that people "are no good." We also talked about some of the scared and angry feelings you may have and some of the ways you may show these feelings to others through your behavior. Now, we will talk about why your parents feel and behave the way they do.

First, we need to know that most of the things that we do, we have learned how to do from someone, usually our parents.

For example, we may like to play baseball or watch it on TV because our parents do. We may have even learned how to catch or hit a ball from our parents showing us, or by watching our parents as they played ball. Sometimes our parents do not try to teach us things directly but we learn anyway by watching their behaviors.

If your parent swears after accidentally breaking a dish, you may learn to swear when your bicycle tire blows. If your parents were spanked by their parents as a punishment for bad behavior, they probably use this form of punishment on you. They learned this is the way to punish children.

You may have learned to "spank" your dog or cat when he behaves badly. If your parents learned to hit you because they are feeling angry, you may have learned from them to hit others because you feel angry, and you may fight a lot in school. So, your parents behave towards you much the same way their parents behaved towards them.

One thing we know for sure is that almost all parents who abuse their children were themselves abused by their parents when they were children.

If your parents are abusive towards you, they probably learned from their parents behavior towards them that they were not loved by them and would not be loved by anyone else. Your parents began to feel that they were "bad" people and that others outside of the family would also hurt them as their parents had. They learned that since they could not trust their own parents not to hurt them, they could not trust anyone else either. People were "just no good!" They felt little and weak and that they had no power to change either their parents' feelings and behaviors or their own. They felt no one else could or would help them. Your parents, when they were children, felt and behaved much as you are feeling and behaving now, and for the same reasons.

15

We talked about these feelings and behaviors in the last chapter. We also talked about the fact that these feelings and behaviors can change if you want them to. You are lucky that you now know this. However, your parents did not know this when they were children. So, now that they are grownups, they still feel and act much the same as they did when they were children. They are still feeling scared and angry much of the time, and that they are bad and that others (including YOU) cannot be trusted and are bad.

Since your parents think of themselves as "bad," and see you as part of themselves, they also think of you as "bad." The behaviors which they think are bad, and see in both themselves and sometimes in the other parent, they will see in you. They may punish themselves and you by doing things which hurt you.

For example, has your Mom ever said to you, "You lie, just like your father"? Or, has Dad ever yelled at you, "Don't ever raise your voice to me again"?

Some parents may punish themselves in other ways. They may marry somebody who will hit them, yell at them a lot, or even not provide them with necessities (food, shelter, clothing). They may turn to drinking alcohol or taking drugs as a way of making themselves feel better. But, this is a SURE punishment, because these things HURT them and those around them.

Your parents may have thought that when you were born you would be the answer to their problems. If they were, as children, taught that they were unloved and not able to get love from anyone; they may have counted on you to give them the love they didn't get from their parents. They wanted you to be their loving parent and take care of them. They may have ex-

16

pected you to act older than you really are (like a grownup), or to stay a little baby. When you didn't do this, your parents may have acted angry with you. They didn't know that you can only be you.

You are not your parents' parent, and you are not a little baby. YOU are YOU — a good person who can give others love, and who needs and can get love from others.

Finally, some parents hurt their children because they are sick (mentally ill) and will hurt themselves and other grownups inside and sometimes outside of the family at times during their illness. Very few parents who abuse their children do so because they are sick mentally (in the mind), and these parents can also be helped to change.

Child Abuse is a problem for many parents and many children in our country. Before we talk about how to solve the problem, we must talk about who "owns" it. Your feelings are your own, and you "own" them. This is true of your parents feelings, too. They "own" their own feelings.

Also, you alone are in control of your behavior. You choose to behave or show others your feelings in a particular way. Your parents also can choose the way in which they show their feelings through their behaviors. Did you know you had a choice when it comes to showing others how you feel? Well, you do!

For example, if you're feeling angry at another kid, you could show him you are angry in a number of different ways. You could:

1) Tell him you are feeling angry at him, and why. (This is probably the best way.)

17

2)   Punch him in the nose.

3)   Steal something of his, to "get even" or "get back" at him.

4)   Hold the angry feeling inside and not *do* anything.

5)   Run away from him.

6)   Punch a pillow and pretend it is he.

Can you think of even more ways you can show your anger? Which way works best for you? Why?

It's important, then, to know that although you may be acting one way now to show others how you feel about how others hurt you, you can CHOOSE to feel and act (behave) in a different way whenever you want to.

To choose to act differently, however, it is important to know who "owns" what part of the problem you have with your parents.

If you leave a dollar on your desk at school, and it is stolen, who owns the problem? Whoever stole the money owns the problem of taking something that belonged to someone else. This is bad behavior. Also, you don't have a dollar anymore. So, you and the person share a problem. He stole something which is yours and which you can no longer have or use. Do you own any part of the problem yourself? Well, unfortunately, most people would agree that it is not a good idea to leave money on a desk at school. By doing so, you were not being helpful to someone who had the problem of taking money that doesn't belong to him.

How is this like the problem of Child Abuse? If you parent is abusing you, that parent owns the problem of showing his feelings with behaviors which hurt others. This is not alright to do and *is* a problem. You share your parents' problem by being hurt. Do you own any part of the problem yourself? Yes, if you are also hurting yourself by choosing to show your scared and angry feelings by behaviors which hurt others, or if you are making it easier for others to keep hurting you, then you do.

For example, if you are choosing to show your scared and angry feelings by fighting (instead of talking about them), grownups outside your family (teachers, neighbors) who can't guess why you're feeling the way you do may be angry at your behavior. While they may not hurt you the way your parents do, they might not give you the help and understanding you need. After a while, you may teach them to give you mainly the kind of attention that makes you feel bad. Of course, if you are still feeling that you are a "bad" person, and that you deserve to (should) be punished, you will make sure you teach grown-ups outside of your family, by behaving badly, to punish you.

Sometimes, the only time your parents pay any attention to you is when they hurt you, and you may feel that even getting hit or yelled at is better than not getting any attention at all. Or your parents may feel so bad after hurting you that they will be extra nice and loving afterward. You may then feel that getting hurt is the price you must pay for being loved. So, you may behave in ways you have been punished for in the past to get this love.

We have talked about the ways in which both you and your parent "own" parts of the abuse problem. In another

19

chapter, we will talk about what you can do to change, what your parents can do to change, and what others outside of your family can do to help you to solve this problem.

CHAPTER III

WHAT CAN BE DONE ABOUT IT?

What can you do to change? What can your parents do to change? How can others outside of your family help you to solve this problem?

Since you have had angry and sad feelings for a long time, and have learned how to show them by behaviors which may hurt you and others, and since your parents have had their own bad feelings which they have shown in hurtful ways for an even longer time, it is very hard to learn new and different ways to feel and behave without some help. Child abuse and child neglect happens all the time and all over the country. It is such a big problem, the government has laws or rules made just for protection, help, and change.

We want to tell you a little more about this. A long, long time ago, parents could do anything they wanted to do to their children. Children were the "property" of their parents. It was okay with the people who lived in the communities of the world (we call this society). It was alright with society if parents gave their children away, put them to work in factories and other jobs, kept their children away from schools, hurt them, or even sold them!

But, that was a long, long time ago. Life has changed in many ways. Society has made many rules, called "laws," to protect children since those days. For instance, children in this country must go to school to learn and no children are allowed to work in jobs that are dangerous to their health. Certainly, parents cannot sell their children! It is against the law for parents to hurt their children's bodies and feelings, on purpose, over and over again. This hurting is called Child Abuse. It is also against the law for parents to *not* take care of their children and for them not to give their children enough food and proper clothing, a safe place to stay, medical care, supervision and protection. If they do not give them all of these, it is called Child Neglect. We talked about these earlier in the book, remember?

One of the laws was made in Washington, D.C., our nation's capital, to keep children all over our country safe. It is called "The Child Abuse Prevention and Treatment Act." It is called *Prevention* because it tries to help stop child abuse and neglect, and it is called *Treatment* because it is also meant to help children who are abused and parents who do abuse, to change.

Did you know that treatment is a way to help with good changes, not a way to catch people and punish them? All fifty states in the United States have their own laws, too, to try to make sure that children are not abused and are not neglected.

These laws also try to help families where there is abuse, to change.

Do you wonder how these laws work? Well, most states have a special office in a big city in their state with a special telephone number for *anyone* to call from *any place* in the state to report (tell about) *any child* they think is being abused or neglected. People can call this number any time during the day or night, any day of the week, and they don't even have to pay for the call. Anyone who thinks a child is being abused or neglected can call. You can call, if you think you or someone you know is being abused or neglected. The number is in the telephone book. Usually it is on the inside of the front cover. If someone wants to call and report, and can't find the number, that person can ask a doctor, teacher, minister or policeman to help get the number.

You might be surprised to know that doctors, teachers, dentists, nurses, school principals, psychologists, social workers and policemen *have* to report any time they think a child is abused or neglected. That is part of the law to protect children and help families. Some of the things that they would have to report if they saw them would be a child who — over and over again — has bruises, burns, cuts or broken bones. They would also have to report a child who is always hungry, skinny and looking for food; or a young child who is out late at night many times without a grownup. Sometimes neighbors call if they see anything like this, and sometimes they call if they hear a lot of yelling, fighting, spanking and screaming. Neighbors don't have to call. They usually call if they are very worried about a child's safety and want to do something to help, but do not know what to do.

When people call this number, they do not have to give their own name — unless they are one of the people we talked about who must report. Callers tell what they have seen and heard, what they are worried about, and the name and address of the child or children. Then, what happens?

Do you remember that in Chapter II we talked about getting help, called "Public Assistance" or "Welfare," from the government if a family does not have enough money for the things everyone needs to live, like food and shelter? Well, every community government has a place where people can go for help with their big problems. This place can be called the Welfare Department, the Department of Public Welfare, or the Department of Social Services. You may have heard of it, by one of these names or another. Some of the people this department helps besides those who do not have enough money for food, clothing and shelter; are people who are crippled, blind, or deaf and need special equipment, rides, and care. Workers from this deparment often help people to learn to use what they do have in a way that is more helpful. These workers can also help by telling people about other places in the community where they can go for help with problems.

Since these Social Service Departments often have the responsibility for (the job of) the protection of children, there is usually a special department to help with problems children are having, or that families are having with children. One of these problems is Child Abuse and Neglect.

There are men and women who work in the special "Children's Department." Their *only* job is to help kids who are, or who are thought to be, abused or neglected by their parents or guardians. These people are called "Child Protective

WHICH PERSON IS FINDING THE GOING EASIER? WHY?

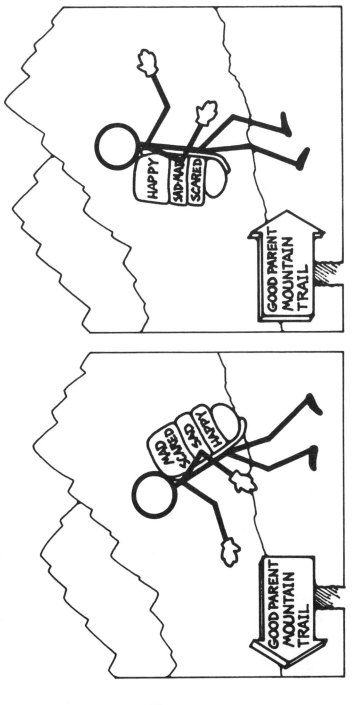

Service Workers." You might hear them called, "C.P.S." workers; which you can see are the initials for their longer name. Do you have a "C.P.S." worker, or a "caseworker"?

C.P.S. workers are especially trained for this important job. They have to know a lot about boys and girls and how they grow, feel and behave. They have to understand how many different kinds of families there are, and how the families act together. They have to know the law, but they are different from policemen. They, also, have to know where the families can go to get more help in changing.

Now, when someone calls to report that she thinks a child is being abused, or neglected, the people at the main state office call and give all the information to the Child Protective Services office in the community where the child or children live. There is a C.P.S. worker "on duty" at all times. It is the law that the worker investigates, or checks, on the child's safety and reports back to the central office right away! To do this the worker must go to the child's home. The worker usually asks many questions. Sometimes this is scary, and sometimes this makes Mom and Dad very mad! We already talked about how parents who are abusing their children have learned not to trust anyone, and think others are "just no darned good!" You might feel the same way. Your parents may be afraid the C.P.S. worker will punish them the way their parents did. They may fear the worker will punish them by taking their children from their home, calling the police to have them arrested, or by just embarrassing them in front of others by making all of this known. Your parents may be very mad at the worker for coming into your home and scaring them. They may be mad at whoever called to tell on them, and they may be angry at you for being the reason for the visit by the worker.

You might be scared you will be hurt by your parents after the worker leaves the house if you said anything, because they were already mad and scared that the worker was there in the first place.

It is very important that you know the C.P.S. worker is there to HELP you and your family, not to punish you and your family. You can TRUST the worker and you can tell the worker the truth, whatever it is. Reports are made about children and families where there is no abuse or neglect and you should say that if it is true. If you are afraid that you will be badly hurt by your parents after the worker leaves the home if you tell the truth, you should tell her that, too. She WILL protect you and she will take steps to help you and your family make changes that will be better for everyone.

The worker can often get all the information she needs in one visit to the child's home, and one talk with the parent, guaradian, and child. There are times when the C.P.S. worker finds there is no reason to believe the child has been abused or neglected. Then the worker sends a written report to the central state office saying this, and all the information about that child is "erased." That is the end of that.

Do you know what happens if the child has been abused or neglected and the worker finds out. The worker will offer *help* to the parents!

There are many different things parents and children can do to solve the problems that are the reasons for a child being abused or neglected. You and your parents can choose to change your feelings and behaviors if you want to. This is a good time to start because the C.P.S. worker can tell you about some of the ways. We'll tell you more about some of them in the next chapter, too. Together, we can all make a plan. With some plans, the child stays right in his or her home with the family, and the worker will check back with them as many times as needed to see if good changes are being made.

If the C.P.S. worker thinks a child is in a dangerous situation, the worker can remove the child from the home. Or, the worker can have a parent removed from the home, but this does not often happen. NO ONE, but a judge, can remove anyone from a home for very long. Even the judge cannot do that until there is a meeting, called a hearing, in the Family Court. The hearing is for parents, the C.P.S. worker, a lawyer for the parents and a lawyer for the children. (Have you ever had your own lawyer?) They all get together to talk to the judge about what has been happening. After the judge has heard from everyone, he decides whether or not the child will live away from his parents. Whenever a child is removed from his home, there is ALWAYS a plan made to help the family get back together again! The C.P.S. worker is the person who checks with the parents and children to see how the plan is working. Sometimes the plan works and the family gets back together soon. Sometimes it does not. Then another plan must be made.

We know that parents can get even more scared and mad, and feel that they are even more "bad" when children are taken from their homes. Kids have these same feelings when this happens. It is important for you to remember that it is not meant as a punishment. It is the first step to keep you safe and for making good changes.

If you are still living with your parents, you probably

wonder what happens to kids who are not. If the judge decides a child would be safer living away from his parents for awhile, the child is usually taken to a Foster Home. Have you ever heard of Foster Homes? They are homes set up for the care and protection of children whose parents are unable to care for them for a certain length of time. A Foster Care Home can be a house or an apartment, and it may have other kids in it, or not. There are usually two Foster Parents, a Foster Mom and a Foster Dad, and they usually have kids of their own. Foster Homes and Foster Parents must have a license from the State government. This means the home is okay and the Foster parents have had special classes to help them to do a good job. Foster parents are paid by the Department of Social Services for caring for Foster children. Foster children get paid, too. They get an allowance.

You probably have a lot more questions about Foster Homes. Children who are going to live in one want to know what it is going to be like. When will they be able to see their own parents? Where? How? Most of all, they want to know when they can go home. Can you think of any other questions about foster care?

Maybe you are in a Foster Home and know the answers to these questions, and a lot more. If not, we'll tell you a little more about Foster Care.

Foster Parents are *not* allowed to hit Foster Children, but, of course, Foster Chidlren are expected to live within the rules of the house and to help with family chores. The workers try very hard to find a good foster home for a child, one that is near his own, so he can stay in the same school. Each child in the home has a bed of his own.

30

Foster Children talk to their parents on the telephone and almost always have visits with them, either in the foster home or in their family home. At first, visits are usually short, but kids can have weekends at home, too. These visits have to be arranged with the parents, the Foster Parents, and the "worker." Of course, there are parents who cannot visit, and some who do not want to visit.

While children are away from their own home they are safe from being hurt by their parents, and they are taken care of with food, shelter, clothes, supervision and protection. This stay not only protects kids it gives boys and girls and their parents a "rest" from the hurting that has been going on. It is a good time to start to change behaviors and feelings that have been hurtful. Parents can get help with the changes and children can get help, too. When the reason that made Foster Care necessary is changed, the child can go home. (This is decided by the judge in Family Court, too, after another hearing.)

A very important word is *change*. The plan is to help with making good changes. How can this be done? We will talk about this in our next chapter.

CHAPTER IV

HOW TO CHANGE?

In another chapter, we talked about how children are protected from harm by the law, and how the laws about Child Abuse and Neglect work. Maybe your family has been seen by a Child Protective Worker to see if you are safe. Many families have been seen in this way. Remember, you can get help for yourself if you are being hurt or neglected by your parents. All you have to do is ask. Tell you teacher, or school nurse, or a friend's parent. Almost any grownup can get you help.

We also talked about FEELINGS, which are inside of you; and BEHAVIORS, which are the way you act to show these feelings. We have talked about how parents sometimes show their scared and angry feelings by behaving in ways which hurt their children. Your parents may have learned not to trust. They have learned to feel bad about themselves, and you; and they have learned to hit and hurt; or to pay no attention to taking care of you. If they act in hurtful ways on purpose, and over and over again, and this is the only way they give you attention, it is called Child Abuse.

You are learning ways to behave from your parents, as they did from theirs, which may be bad. But you are not bad! Children who have been abused get scared and angry feelings, which they may show by behaving in some ways which are hurtful to themselves. Do you often hit, yell, swear, push and fight with other children at home or at play? Do you yell, fight, run around and not sit still and not pay attention at school?

Anyone and everyone can change his feelings and behaviors if he CHOOSES. You and your parents can learn new and different ways to feel and behave, which are not hurtful. This is change. You know you can choose to change.

To make changes you have to know who "owns" the problem. We talked earlier about the problem of "ownership," and about the part of the problem you have with your parents, which you owned. You should know that you can only change the part of the problem you own, which means your behavior. You cannot change the part of the problem your parents own, which means their behavior. They have to do this themselves. You do not have control over what others do.

What are some of the behaviors you own which you can change? Do you sometimes show your scared and angry feelings by fighting and yelling? Do you often do just the opposite of what parents or teachers ask you to do? Do you act like a baby even though you are not a baby anymore, or behave like a grownup most of the time even though you are still a child? Do you cry most of the time, or not at all? Can you think of any ways you show your scared or angry feelings which hurt others, or make it easier for others to hurt you?

If you behave in any of these ways with your parents, they will probably continue to hurt you — your body or your feelings. If you act in any of these ways most of the time with other children, they probably will not want to be your friend. They may hit back, call you names, or stay away from you and not play with you. You will teach them to behave in ways that make you feel "bad." If you choose to act in any of these ways with grownups outside of your family — teachers, neighbors, parents of friends — they may not understand your behavior and get angry. They may not hurt you the way your parents do, but they may punish you, and may not be able to help you. You will teach them to give you the kind of attention that makes you feel bad. And, you are not bad!

Now that you know it is possible to choose to change, and what part of the problem you own — YOUR feelings and behaviors that hurt others or help others hurt you, you can start to change.

You will need to TRUST someone outside of your family to help you learn new ways of feeling and behaving. Teachers, guidance counselors, school nurses, ministers and priest, caseworkers, forster care workers, social workers and psychologists are some of the people you can trust. Maybe you can think of some more people you can trust.

Sometimes it is very hard to believe that other people will not hurt you. You might be afraid to take the chance. You might feel all alone. Try not to be afraid. Ask for help. No matter how willing people are to help, they cannot know how bad you feel, or how much you want help, unless you ask

35

WHAT IS THIS CHILD PROBABLY FEELING AND THINKING?

HOW CAN HE GET HELP?

them. Let other people help you. Many people care about you.

We will now talk about some ways you can change. You have learned how to feel and behave. You can learn new ways to "relate" (that means to be with, get along with, and behave with people) that you can use with others. People must "relate" with others all their lives. You relate to your parents, sisters and brothers, neighbors, friends, schoolmates, teachers, storekeepers, and many other people, right now. Someday you may relate to husbands and wives, bosses, co-workers, and maybe your own children.

The people you decided to trust can help you learn new ways to relate. They can make sure you have protection, necessities for living, and chances to learn ways to feel and behave that may make you feel "good." We know some of you who are reading this book are already getting this from child protective workers, foster care workers, and counselors; in special classes, play groups, nursery schools, social groups and therapy groups.

"Counseling" and "Therapy" are words used to describe (tell) what happens when you talk about your problems and what to do about them with a caring, specially trained person who can help you change. There are many different names for these people. Some of the names are: therapist, doctor, social worker, psychologist, and psychiatrist. These people all have to "act in your best interest," which means many things about taking care of you. One is that counselors keep what you say to them secret.

Talking with a counselor about scared and angry feelings and behaviors, and what happens to you when you behave in these old ways, can help you feel better about yourself. It is a good step to take for finding new ways to act that are not hurtful to you. A counselor might come to your home to talk, or you might go to the counselor's office. You might talk to the counselor by yourself, or with your parents, or with the whole family, or even with your teacher. You might see a counselor with a group of other children, or with a group of other families who have some of the same problems. Sometimes counselors play games, or take you on outings — alone, or with other boys and girls. This can be fun! It helps you to learn to trust, which is a new way to feel. Being with a group of other children helps you to see how your old behaviors are hurtful to you. You have a chance to practice new behavior you have talked about with your counselor. You have a chance to relate to others in new and changed ways.

Here is an example of what we have been talking about: We knew a child who wanted very much to get attention from his teacher and classmates. What he did was to act the same way as he had learned to behave at home. He yelled out of turn, he used swear words with the kids and with the teacher, and he fought a lot. Did this get him attention? Yes! What kind? The attention he got from the teacher was punishment. The attention he got from his classmates was that no one would play with him. By talking with the therapist he learned that he could behave in different ways to get attention that made him feel good about himself. What do you think that he could have done differently?

Now you know you can choose to change, and how to make changes. You might be wondering about your parents. They can choose to change and get help to change, too, the same way you can. Know there is a problem, know change is possible, trust others to help, ask for help, and with this help learn new ways to feel and behave.

Parents can get help to feel better about themselves from many people just as you can. The Child Protective Worker can help your parents find out where to go to get help with medical problems, money problems, transportation problems, child care problems, and other problems which make being a parent a very difficult job for them. The worker's caring for your parents can help them begin to trust others. When parents feel better about themselves, they usually feel better about their children, and are less likely to use abusive behaviors with their children.

Parents can get help to change ways in taking care of their children, right in their own homes, from specially trained people like public health nurses, homemaker aides, or parent aides. All of these people can help explain to parents what their children need at different ages, how their children might act, and how parents might treat their children, in caring ways. These helpers might tell parents how to do these and other things, or they might actually show them how. They can help by acting like "good" parents to your parents.

Outside of the home, too, your parents can get help to change at special classes on how to be a good parent. They can get help from nursery school and day care centers, which are places where children can go for a few hours to play safely so that parents have some time for themselves to rest, go to work, or do something they would like to do. Parents can get help from a counselor or therapist who will talk with them about the ways they have behaved which have hurt themselves and you. Parents can also be helped to learn new ways to behave.

Best of all, they can join a group of other parents who have the same problem. This group is called "Parents Anonymous" or P.A. Parents Anonymous was started by a mother who wanted to stop abusing her children. P.A. was started in California, and has spread to other states and other countries. Why? Because it is such a good idea!

At a Parents Anonymous meeting, moms and dads who want to stop hurting their children talk about their problems with other parents who have the same problems, and with a person who does not have a problem with hurting his children. This person is called a "sponsor," and knows about other places in the community where parents and children can get different kinds of help.

Parents in these groups only have to use their first names. At first, it is hard to trust other people. After going to some of these meetings, sharing worries and feelings, and getting new ideas from one another; the parents often become friends. Sometimes the group becomes like a family, because the parents in the group learn to trust one another and to really care for one another. As they give and get caring, it is easier for them to give caring to their children.

We've talked about how you can change and how your parents can change. Now, let's talk about "endings." Happy endings, and not so happy endings!

Happy endings happen when all the members of your family want to change, choose to change, and have gotten help in changing. Not so happy endings happen when some members of your family cannot, or will not, choose to change.

It is important to remember that no matter what anyone else does, YOU can CHOOSE TO CHANGE YOUR OWN

BEHAVIOR AND FEELINGS. You can choose to ASK FOR HELP. YOU can CHOOSE TO FEEL GOOD!

CHAPTER V

ANSWERS TO THE PICTURE QUESTIONS

Picture on Page 11

Question: Both Parents Are Hurting Their Kids. Which One Is Doing It On Purpose?

Answer: You are right if you said that the parent who is spanking his kid is hurting him on purpose, as a punishment. The other parent is also hurting her child as she cleans out his cut, but she is not hurting him on purpose.

Question: Which Parent Is A Child Abuser?

Answer: This is a hard question. You're right if you said

43

you couldn't tell from the picture. Many parents spank their children as a punishment and almost all parents hurt their children's bodies or feelings accidentally or on purpose at times in their lives. Remember, Child Abuse is when parents or guardians hurt their children's bodies or feelings over and over again on purpose, and the *only* way such parents give a child attention is by yelling at him, hitting him, or being angry at him.

Picture on Page 15

Question: What Is This Child Learning To Do Through His Father's Behavior Toward Him?

Answer: This child has learned that when he is feeling angry at someone he shows he is feeling angry by yelling, swearing and threatening. So, this child has learned certain behaviors to use with certain feelings. As you've read, you can learn to choose other behaviors to use with your angry feelings.

Picture on Page 25

Question: Which Person Is Finding The Going Easier? Why?

Answer: Every person carries around a load of feelings. While both parents have the same kinds of feelings, the parent on the right has Happy Feelings as his biggest load, and Scared Feelings as his smallest load. The parent on the left is finding the going rough. It is very hard to do things when carrying around a big load of scared and mad feelings.

What's in your backpack?

Picture on Page 29

Question: What Are These Parents Probably Thinking and Feeling?

Answer: These parents are feeling mad at being bothered, and scared that they will get into trouble for their behavior.

Question: What Is This Child Probably Thinking and Feeling?

Answer: This child is feeling scared that he may get into trouble, or that his parents might, if he tells the worker the truth.

Question: What Is This Child Probably Feeling and Thinking? How Can He Get Help?

Answer: This child is probably feeling scared and all alone. He can help himself by opening the door — that is — by trusting someone outside of his family enough to talk about his problems with them and to ask for their help.

Remember, there are many people who care about you, would like to help you, and can help you. They can only help you if you ask for help!

REFERENCES

REFERENCES

For Children and Parents

Gardener, *The Boys and Girls Book About Divorce*, 1970. Bantam Press, New York, New York.

>This is an excellent book for children whose parents are divorced or separated.

Freed, *T.A. for Tots*. Volume I, 1973.
T.A. for Tots. Volume II, 1980.
T.A. for Kids, 1977. Jalmar Press, Sacramento, California

>These are fun and they are useful books for kids and their parents to read.

For Parents

Parents Anonymous. National Headquarters: 22330 Hawthorne Boulevard, Suite 208, Torrance, California 90505

> Toll free telephone number from anywhere in the country, except California, is 1-800-421-0352. (In California it is 1-800-352-0386).

> You can call the national number, given above, and they will refer you to the local chapter in your city or state.

> Many states have "Hot Lines" for Crisis Referral. For example, in New York State, the number would be 1-800-462-6406 for such referral. It operates any day and any hour. Remember, this help is free and you may remain anonymous when you call.

Ginott, *Between Parent and Child*, 1965.
Between Parent and Teenager, 1969. The Macmillan Company, New York.

> These are excellent books for parents who want to learn to improve communication with their children and adolescents.

Becker, *Parents Are Teachers*, 1971. Research Press, Champaign, Illinois.

Patterson, *Living With Children*, 1976. Research Press, Champaign, Illinois.

These are good basic books on Behavior Modification principles and techniques.

For Professionals

Herbruck, *Breaking the Cycle of Child Abuse*. 1979. Winston Press, Minneapolis, Minnesota.